Picture Books for
Inclusive Classroom

Teaching Children About People with Special Needs

Written by Cynthia G. Costello

Illustrated by Kay McCabe

Fearon Teacher Aids

A Division of Frank Schaffer Publications. Inc.

THIS BOOK BELONGS TO
MR. & MRS. ULPH
(TIMOTHY & VICKIE)
PLEASE HANDLE WITH CARE

Editors: Maria Backus, Stephanie Oberc-Garcia, Christine Hood
Cover Design: Riley Wilkinson
Book Design: Good Neighbor Press, Inc.

© Fearon Teacher Aids

A Division of Frank Schaffer Publications, Inc.
23740 Hawthorne Boulevard
Torrance, CA 90505-5927

Fearon Teacher Aids products were formerly manufactured and distributed by American Teaching Aids, Inc., a subsidiary of Silver Burdett Ginn, and are now manufactured and distributed by Frank Schaffer Publications, Inc. FEARON, FEARON TEACHER AIDS, and the FEARON balloon logo are marks used under license from Simon & Schuster, Inc.

Table of Contents

Introduction 7

Literature Units

A Picture Book of Helen Keller by David A. Adler 8
    Helen Keller: Before and After Anne Sullivan (Moderate) 11
    An Award for Helen Keller (Moderate) 12
    Famous Quotations (Difficult) 13

Mom Can't See Me by Sally Hobart Alexander 14
    The Case of the Missing Guide Dog (Easy) 17
    The Same, but Different (Moderate) 18

Russell Is Extra Special: A Book About Autism for Children
by Charles A. Amenta, III, M.D. 19
    What's the Problem? (Easy) 22
    Keeping a Schedule (Moderate) 23

A Guide Dog Puppy Grows Up by Caroline Arnold 24
    A Puppy in Training (Easy) 27
    Lead the Way, Honey (Easy) 28

Our Brother Has Down's Syndrome by Shelley Cairo 29
    Vocabulary Activity 32
    Research Summary (Moderate) 33

Arnie and the New Kid by Nancy Carlson 34
    Visiting a Friend (Easy) 37
    Write a Letter (Difficult) 38

Harry and Willy and Carrothead by Judith Caseley 39
    Things to Do (Moderate) 42
    A Story of Friends (Difficult) 43

What Do You Mean I Have a Learning Disability?
by Kathleen M. Dwyer 44
    Be the Teacher (Moderate) 47
    Jimmy's Secrets (Difficult) 48

What Do You Mean I Have Attention Deficit Disorder?
by Kathleen M. Dwyer 49
    Take-Home Checklist 52
    Getting Ready for School (Easy) 53

Helping Hands by Suzanne Haldane 54
    A Capuchin Monkey at Work: Make a Mini-Book (Easy) 57
    Capuchin Monkeys in the Wild (Difficult) 58

Silent Lotus by Jeanne M. Lee 59
    Lots About Lotus (Moderate) 62
    Story Web (Difficult) 63

Knots on a Counting Rope by Bill Martin, Jr. and John Archambault 64
    Break the Code (Easy) 67
    What Is a Color? (Moderate) 68

Summer Tunes: A Martha's Vineyard Vacation by Patricia McMahon 69
    Our Photo Albums (Easy) 72
    Alike and Different (Moderate) 73
    Ice-Cream Time (Moderate) 74

Imagine Me on a Sit-Ski! by George Moran 75
    What You Need on a Sit-Ski (Easy) 78

Beethoven Lives Upstairs by Barbara Nichol 79
    Neighborly Thoughts (Moderate) 82

My Buddy by Audrey Osofsky 83
    Buddy's Backpack (Moderate) 86
    Compound Words (Difficult) 87

***Our Teacher's in a Wheelchair* by Mary Ellen Powers** **88**

    Yes, I Can! (Easy) 90

***The Balancing Girl* by Berniece Rabe** **91**

    At the School Carnival (Easy) 94

***Alex Is My Friend* by Marisabina Russo** **95**

    Puzzle Time (Moderate) 98

    Puppet Time (Moderate) 99

    Comparisons (Difficult) 100

***Ruby Mae Has Something to Say* by David Small** **101**

    Your Invention (Moderate) 104

    Character Words (Difficult) 105

Appendices

    Appendix A: The Manual Alphabet 106

    Appendix B: The Braille Alphabet 107

    Appendix C: Resources 108

    Appendix D: Bibliography 109

    Appendix E: Book Information 110

    Appendix F: Additional Books 111

Introduction

Picture Books for an Inclusive Classroom provides complete literature units for 20 books that focus on a variety of special needs. Through these fiction and nonfiction titles, your students will begin to understand that all people can lead happy, successful lives, regardless of their challenges. This book is designed to increase your students' awareness and appreciation of people with special needs, while providing classroom activities in reading, writing, language, social studies, math, and science.

For each title, you will find:

◆ a story summary highlighting the special need

◆ a vocabulary list

◆ a vocabulary activity to complete *after* you read the book with students

◆ questions to discuss *before, during*, and *after* you read the book with students

◆ extension activities across the curriculum that foster an awareness of and sensitivity to the special needs and challenges many people face, as well as encourage friendship among all students

◆ a home or community connection to extend classroom learning

◆ activity sheets to hone skills at different levels

As you share the books with children, help them realize that the physical and mental challenges people face need not exclude them from living full, independent lives. Children will discover how the people in these books have overcome their disabilities, and sometimes their fears. Through reading and hands-on explorations, students will realize that what makes us different also makes us special.

A Picture Book of Helen Keller

by David A. Adler
Publisher: Holiday House, 1991
Type: Nonfiction

Book Summary

This book tells the inspiring story of Helen Keller. Before she was two years old, Helen Keller lost her eyesight and hearing to a high fever. She was an unhappy child, until her family hired Anne Sullivan as her live-in teacher. With Anne Sullivan's help, Helen learned to read Braille and speak so that others could understand her. She attended college, became politically active, wrote an autobiography, and received the Presidential Medal of Freedom from President Lyndon Johnson in 1964.

Vocabulary

blind	deaf	handicapped	manners	pantry	soul
companion	fever	lectured	mischievous	pretended	

Vocabulary Activity

Divide the class into groups of three. Provide each group with paper, glue, and letter-shaped pasta or alphabet cereal. Ask each group to select five words from the vocabulary list. Instruct them to use the pasta or cereal letters to spell the words correctly and glue them to the paper. Display the results. Ask students how they think this method of presenting words might be helpful for someone like Helen Keller. Which senses did Helen Keller rely on? Which sense does this method of lettering use in order to "read"?

Discussion Questions

Discuss these questions *before* you read the book with students:

◆ Have you ever heard of Helen Keller? What do you know about her?

◆ Look at the illustrations in the book. How do you think Helen's special needs affected her parents and family life? What generalizations can you make about her home life from studying the illustrations in the book?

Discuss these questions *while* you read the book with students:

◆ How did Helen feel about being blind and deaf before accepting help from Anne Sullivan? How would you have felt? What would you have done?

◆ What was Helen's first word? Explain how she learned it.

Discuss these questions *after* you read the book with students:

◆ How do you think medicines were different in 1880 than they are today? What kind of help is available for blind and deaf people today that was unknown in 1880?

◆ What special problems do you think Helen experienced while attending college? Why did she need a human companion? Why was a guide dog inadequate?

◆ Would you have wanted to be Helen Keller's companion? Describe what would have been rewarding about it. What would have been a challenge?

◆ Which of your senses do you think you would miss most? Which of your five senses is the least important to you? Explain your thoughts.

Extension Activities

Geography: Ask students to locate Tuscumbia, Alabama, on a map of the United States. Ask them to figure out the distance between Tuscumbia and their own communities.

Small-Motor Skills: Encourage students to improvise simple hand signals that express their needs and wants. For example, how could they tell someone that they are hungry? that they don't feel well? that they are tired? Help students learn the finger alphabet that Anne Sullivan taught Helen Keller. Which method is more efficient and easily understood? You might also share with students *Finger Spelling Fun* by David Adler (Watts, 1980) or *The Handmade Alphabet* by Laura Rankin (Dial, 1991).

Biography: Suggest that students learn more about Alexander Graham Bell. Encourage them to read the book *Dear Dr. Bell . . . Your Friend, Helen Keller* by Judith St. George (Putnam, 1992) for further information about the friendship between Helen Keller and Alexander Graham Bell.

Critical Thinking: Create a "feely" box by cutting a hole in the top of a box that is big enough for a child's hand to fit through. Place common objects inside the box for children to identify, such as a spoon, toy car, stuffed animal, cotton ball, rubber ball, and paper cup. Have children take turns placing their hands through the hole to feel the objects inside. Can they figure out what each object is? Write down or ask a volunteer to write down their ideas. Then open the box to reveal the objects. Encourage students to talk about the experience. Did they find it easy or difficult to rely on their sense of touch? What do they imagine it would be like to rely on the sense of touch all the time?

Home Connection

Have students ask five people in their family or neighborhood if they believe it would be more difficult being blind or deaf. Have students report their results to the class. Then make a graph showing the combined results.

Activity Sheets

Helen Keller: Before and After Anne Sullivan
Skill Level: Moderate
Have students make a two-column chart describing what Helen Keller was like before and after the arrival of Anne Sullivan.

An Award for Helen Keller
Skill Level: Moderate
Have students design an award for Helen Keller and write an acceptance speech she might give.

Famous Quotations
Skill Level: Difficult
Before students complete this activity sheet, share the book *Helen Keller* by Lois Markham (Watts, 1993).

Name _____

Helen Keller: Before and After Anne Sullivan

Think about what Helen Keller was like before her teacher, Anne Sullivan, arrived. What was Helen Keller like after she arrived? Fill in the chart below with your ideas.

Helen Keller before Anne Sullivan	Helen Keller after Anne Sullivan

Name _____

An Award for Helen Keller

Helen Keller received many awards throughout her life. Create an award for Helen Keller below.

To: _____

For: _____

_____

_____

Write an acceptance speech from Helen Keller.

_____

_____

_____

_____

_____

Name _____

Famous Quotations

Helen Keller met many famous people. What do you think they said about her? Write what you think they might have said on the lines. Don't forget to use quotation marks!

Teacher Anne Sullivan

_____

_____

_____

_____

Writer Mark Twain

_____

_____

_____

_____

President Lyndon Johnson

_____

_____

_____

Actress Patty Duke

_____

_____

_____

Scientist Albert Einstein

_____

_____

_____

President Franklin Delano Roosevelt

_____

_____

_____

Mom Can't See Me

by Sally Hobart Alexander
Publisher: Macmillan, 1990
Type: Nonfiction

Book Summary

In this book, students are introduced to Leslie, a nine-year-old girl, who tells the story of her mother who is blind, yet living a very active and productive life. The mother, Sally Hobart Alexander, is also the author of the book.

Vocabulary

blotches	cringe	gymnastics	rude
blurry	designated	harness	translator
Braille	duets	inherit	
cassette	embarrassed	interrupt	

Vocabulary Activity

Have students work in pairs. Suggest that one partner pretend to be blind, while the other student is sighted. Ask the sighted student to read each vocabulary word to his or her "blind" partner. The "blind" student listens to each word and uses it in a sentence. Then have partners trade roles.

Discussion Questions

Discuss these questions *before* you read the book with students:

◆ In what ways would your life be different if your mother or father were blind? In what ways would you need to help at home?

Discuss these questions *while* you read the book with students:

◆ Why does Leslie's mother wear sunglasses?

◆ How does Leslie's mother use her other senses to compensate for her loss of vision?

◆ What did Leslie's mother do when she realized she was going blind?

◆ Who is Marit?

◆ What work did Leslie's mother do before she became blind? What does she do now?

◆ What do you think Leslie wishes for when she blows out her birthday candles?

Discuss these questions *after* you read the book with students:

◆ Should Leslie and Joel worry about "catching" blindness from their mother? Why or why not?

◆ Give an example of a possible problem that might occur if your mother went blind.

Extension Activities

Listening Skills: Record the story (or another story) on cassette tape. Ask students to listen closely to the story the way a blind student would.

Real-life Experience: With adequate supervision, let students work in pairs to experience what it might be like to be blind. One student can use a blindfold and cane; the other student guides the blindfolded student through the hallway. Then have children switch roles. Afterwards, discuss the experience. Which senses did children rely on? How did the experience make them feel?

Health/Science: Invite a health professional to your class to discuss eye care and first aid. Ahead of time, ask students to write down questions they would like to ask the speaker, including questions based on the book. Afterward, you can discuss the functions of each part of the eye with your class.

Critical Thinking: Place several similar objects on a tray, such as a pencil, pen, crayon, marker, and paintbrush. Cover the tray with a cloth. Then invite students to slip a hand under the cloth to feel the objects. Point out that all the objects have the same basic shape. How can they distinguish one object from another? As students identify each one, have them describe which features helped them name it.

Oral Language/Listening Skills: Choose a community landmark well known to students, such as a statue in a park, a building, or a store front. Tell students to close their eyes and picture the landmark you are describing. When students think they know what it is, tell them to identify it. Then, working in pairs, have students take turns describing other landmarks to each other. Suggest that they imagine they are describing the landmarks for Leslie's mother. Which words would help her "see" the landmarks in her mind?

Real-life Experience/Spelling: Remind students that the Braille alphabet is a special system of raised dots by which blind people read. Reproduce the Braille alphabet (Appendix B, page 107) and give it to the class. Encourage students to print short messages to friends using the Braille system. To create raised dots, show students how to push pen tips carefully through heavy paper. Remind students to make a space between each letter and a double space between words. Challenge them to feel the dots on the raised side of the paper to "read" the words. Remember that when the paper is turned over the words will be in reverse.

Home Connection

Ask students to write short stories about their relationships with their mothers, fathers, or other primary caregivers. Invite them to illustrate their stories, showing the things they do together.

Activity Sheets

The Case of the Missing Guide Dog
Skill Level: Easy
Have students cut out the pictures of guide dogs and glue them in the correct boxes.

The Same, but Different
Skill Level: Moderate
Have students use a Venn diagram to compare and contrast activities for a blind mom and a sighted mom.

Name _____

The Case of the Missing Guide Dog

Look at the pictures below. What is missing? Cut out the guide dogs at the bottom of the page. Glue each in the correct box.

The guide dog is leading the woman down the street.

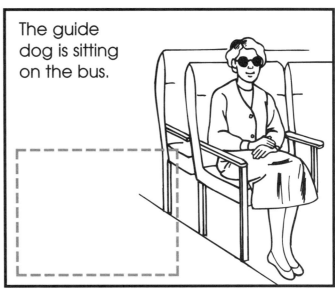

The guide dog is sitting on the bus.

The guide dog is sleeping.

The guide dog is playing.

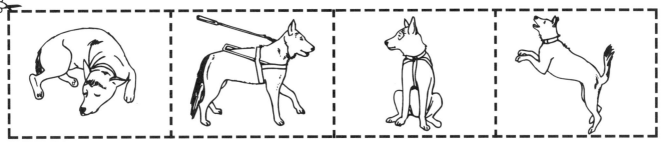

Reproducible

Name _____

The Same, but Different

A Venn diagram can help you compare two people or objects. The gray area in the middle tells you what the people or objects have in common. The other circles tell you how the items are different from each other.

Read the phrases in the box below. Write them in the correct section of the Venn diagram.

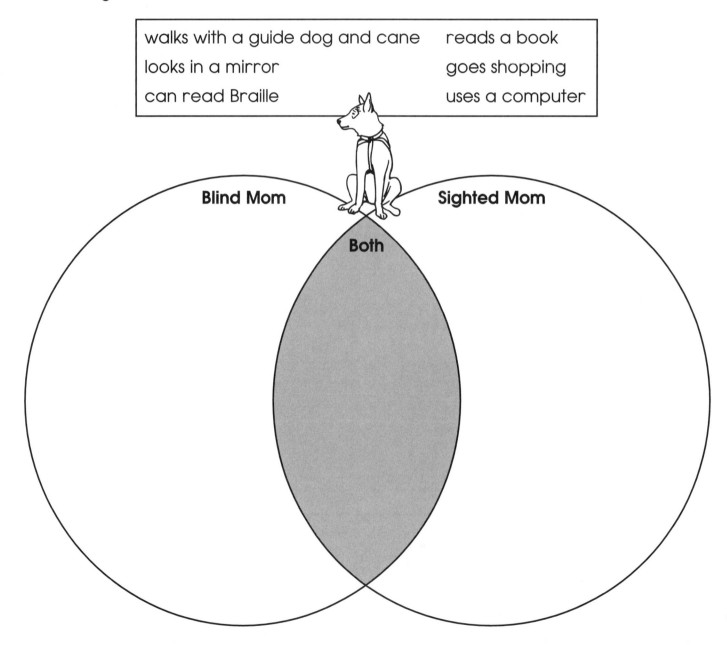

walks with a guide dog and cane	reads a book
looks in a mirror	goes shopping
can read Braille	uses a computer

Blind Mom   **Sighted Mom**

Both

Russell Is Extra Special: A Book About Autism for Children

by Charles A. Amenta III, M.D.
Publisher: Magination Press, 1992
Type: Nonfiction

Book Summary

This book offers a look at family life with a severely autistic child. It is the story of Russell, a happy child, with specific likes, dislikes, needs, wants, and abilities, as recorded by his physician father. The characteristics of autism are explained honestly and thoroughly. The book includes a somewhat technical introduction and bibliography for adults.

Vocabulary

autism	cuddle	imitate	severely
autistic	difficulty	language	tantrum
clumsy	echo	rewards	
comfortable	ignore	robot	

Vocabulary Activity

Challenge students to use the vocabulary words in sentences, either orally or written, that indicate an understanding of autism. Encourage more advanced students to incorporate the words into short stories about a fictional child with the disorder. You might also suggest that they write sequels to Russell's story.

Discussion Questions

Discuss these questions *before* you read the book with students:

◆ How would you feel if you could not speak? What problems might you have?

Discuss these questions *while* you read the book with students:

◆ In which three ways is Russell different from other children?

◆ How does Russell play? What "toys" does he prefer?

◆ What kinds of things make Russell unhappy? How does Russell react when he is unhappy? What makes you unhappy? How do you react? Discuss similarities and differences.

Discuss these questions *after* you read the book with students:

◆ How do Russell's family members help him? How is raising Russell different than raising his brothers?

◆ How important is it to have friends? to be a friend? How could you be a friend to an autistic child?

Extension Activities

Real-life Experience: Challenge several students to spend 15 minutes without speaking. Then discuss the experience as a class. How were the students able to make their wants and needs known? How did they interact with their classmates? Conclude by discussing how important language is for communication.

Math: Remind students that Russell needs to keep a regular schedule. Point out that students often keep regular schedules, too. With the class, choose five events from the school day that always happen at the same time. Encourage students to draw clocks for each event to show at what time it occurs.

Letter Writing: Encourage the class to learn more about autism. What questions do they have about it? Explain that one way to have their questions answered is to write to an expert in the field. Invite students to dictate a letter to you that includes questions they have about autism. Then send the letter to:

Autism Society of America
7910 Woodmount Avenue, Suite 300
Bethesda, MD 00814-3015

Share the response with the class.

Home Connection

Explain to students that autistic children are often extremely sensitive to sights, sounds, and smells. Ask students to look around their homes and list ten items that might be unpleasant or cause a problem for an autistic child, even though the item is not a problem for them.

Activity Sheets

What's the Problem?
Skill Level: Easy
Have students cross out five things in the picture that might cause a problem for Russell.

Keeping a Schedule
Skill Level: Moderate
Have students draw pictures or write about six things they do each day at school on a regular schedule.

Name _____

What's the Problem?

Look at the picture below. Cross out five things in the picture that might be a problem for Russell.

Name _____

Keeping a Schedule

Russell likes to keep a regular schedule. You probably keep a regular schedule, too. List or draw pictures of six things that you do at school each day on a regular schedule. Number them in the order in which you do them.

A Guide Dog Puppy Grows Up

by Caroline Arnold
Publisher: Harcourt, Brace, Jovanovich, 1991
Type: Nonfiction

Book Summary

Many guide dogs spend their early days with a family. Amy and her family are raising Honey, a golden retriever puppy, to become a guide dog. The story shows the training the dogs must go through and the necessary requirements for guide dogs and their owners.

Vocabulary

barrier	destination	harness	rural
campus	dormitory	kennel	suburban
ceremonies	extensive	pamphlet	veterinarian
commands	formal	retriever	volunteer
corridor	guide		

Vocabulary Activity

Show students several examples of pamphlets. Explain that a pamphlet gives people information about a topic. Let children note the style and format of the pamphlets. Then ask students to create a pamphlet to inform people about guide dogs. As children write and illustrate their pamphlets, encourage them to use as many vocabulary words as possible.

Discussion Questions

Discuss these questions *before* you read the book with students:

◆ What do you know about guide dogs?

◆ Do you know anyone who has a guide dog?

◆ How does a guide dog help someone who is blind?

Discuss these questions *while* you read the book with students:

◆ How are guide dog puppies selected? Which characteristics are most important?

◆ What special training must Amy give her guide dog puppy?

◆ How does Honey change as she grows?

◆ What training does Honey receive at Guide Dogs for the Blind, Inc.? How long is she there? How long does she train with Anne?

◆ Who is Anne Gelles? What is her career?

Discuss these questions *after* you read the book with students:

◆ Do you think Honey enjoys her work? Explain your ideas.

◆ Why don't all blind people use guide dogs? What aids do they use instead?

◆ What is "intelligent disobedience"? Why is it sometimes necessary for Honey to disobey?

Extension Activities

Research/Comparing/Drawing Conclusions: Have students check reference books for information about golden retrievers, Labrador retrievers, and German shepherds. Then ask the students to make charts noting the characteristics these dogs have in common. Ask students to draw conclusions about why these breeds make good guide dogs.

Art/Writing: How do children think Honey will help Anne? Brainstorm ideas with the class. Assign each idea to partners. Invite partners to draw pictures of Honey and Anne in that situation. Encourage them to write sentences, too. Then bind the pages together into a book. Tell children that they have created a sequel to *A Guide Dog Puppy Grows Up*. Ask them to name their new book. Write and decorate the class title and staple it to the front of the book.

Art/Writing: Remind students that the citizens of San Rafael, California, are used to seeing guide dogs on their streets. Discuss with students what sighted people should do when they see a guide dog. How can students identify a guide dog that is working? After the discussion, have students design and illustrate information posters about guide dogs. Display the posters around the school for others to see.

Letter Writing: Ask students what additional information they would like to learn about guide dogs. List their questions on the chalkboard. Then write a class letter incorporating their questions. Send the letter to:

Guide Dogs for the Blind, Inc.
P.O. Box 151200
San Rafael, California 94915-1200

Share the response with the class.

Home Connection

Invite students to research a dog breed they would like to own. Have them list five reasons, explaining their choices. Then brainstorm and list things their new dogs will need, such as *food, love, exercise,* and so on. Ask children if they think they are ready to be responsible pet owners, and why.

Activity Sheets

A Puppy in Training
Skill Level: Easy
Have students cut apart the pictures on the activity sheet. Then place the pictures in order and staple them to make a mini-book about guide dogs.

Lead the Way, Honey
Skill Level: Moderate
Have students draw a line showing how Honey helps lead Anne safely around the neighborhood.

© Fearon Teacher Aids FE10001

Name _____

A Puppy in Training

Cut apart the pictures. Staple them in the correct order to make a mini-book about guide dogs.

Name _____

Lead the Way, Honey

Draw a line to help Honey lead Anne safely down the sidewalk to the grocery store.

Our Brother Has Down's Syndrome

by Shelley Cairo
Publisher: Firefly Books, 1985
Type: Nonfiction

Book Summary

Two sisters, Jasmine and Tara, share the story of their brother, Jai, who has Down's syndrome. Through factual information and family photographs, they convey how Jai is similar to other children.

Vocabulary

attention	different	retarded
cells	Down's syndrome	special
chromosomes	microscope	

Vocabulary Activity

Cut apart the words and word shapes on the activity sheet (page 32). Glue them onto index cards. Mix up the cards, then challenge children to match each vocabulary word to its word shape. Children can also draw the word shapes for the vocabulary words on the chalkboard.

Discussion Questions

Discuss these questions *before* you read the book with students:

◆ What is Down's syndrome?

◆ Can you catch Down's syndrome, like other illnesses? Is there a way to cure it? Define and explore children's answers.

Discuss these questions *while* you read the book with students:

◆ How is Jai different from other children his age? How is he the same?

◆ What does Jai learn at play group? What does his teacher do when she makes a home visit?

◆ How would you feel about living with Jai? What generalizations can you make about Jai's sisters and the way they accept him?

Discuss these questions *after* you read the book with students:

◆ Why do Jasmine and Tara want to share their story with others? What can you learn from their story? Why is this important?

◆ How is the word *retarded* handled in the book? What should you do if you hear someone calling another child retarded?

◆ How could you help children with Down's syndrome at school or in your community?

Extension Activities

Art/Self-esteem: Recall that one of the main purposes of this book is to acknowledge that everyone is special. Provide students with art supplies, and ask them to create a badge to express why all children are special. Encourage children to exchange their badges with classmates.

Literature Connection: Share the book *Be Good to Eddie Lee* by Virginia Fleming (Philomel, 1993). It is a fictional story about feelings, honesty, and the sensitivity of Down's syndrome children. As you read the story with the class, encourage children to compare details in this book with details from Jai's story.

Letter Writing: Ask students to list questions they may have about Down's syndrome. Then write a letter with the class to the National Down's Syndrome Society for more information. In your letter, mention the books the class is reading. Send the letter to:

The National Down Syndrome Society
666 Broadway
New York, New York 10012

Share the response with the class.

Home Connection

Invite students to draw pictures of their families. Suggest that they illustrate something specific their families like to do together. Encourage each student to write a caption under the picture that includes names of family members. Display children's drawings on a bulletin board titled, *Families Are Special.*

Activity Sheets

Vocabulary Activity

This activity sheet is used for the vocabulary activity on page 29.

Research Summary

Skill Level: Moderate

Have students research information about Down's syndrome to complete this activity sheet.

Name _____

Vocabulary Activity

Cut apart the words and word shapes. Glue each to an index card. Match the word with its word shape.

cells	
special	
different	
family	
brother	
sister	
microscope	
chromosomes	

Name _____

Research Summary

Describe what you have you learned about Down's syndrome by completing the sentences below.

I have learned how people get Down's syndrome. They _____

_____

_____

_____

I have learned how Down's syndrome children are just like me. They _____

_____

_____

_____

They are different from me in some ways, too. They _____

_____

_____

_____

From my research, I have learned that _____

_____

_____

_____

_____

Arnie and the New Kid

by Nancy Carlson
Publisher: Puffin, 1992
Type: Fiction

Book Summary

Philip, the new kid at school, is in a wheelchair. Arnie teases Philip until Arnie breaks his leg in a fall. Then Arnie experiences a similar lack of mobility. With Arnie's new understanding, he becomes friends with Philip.

Vocabulary

challenged	discovered	hospital	teased
coach	emergency	rushed	twisted
complained	finished	sprained	

Vocabulary Activity

Write the vocabulary words on the chalkboard. Ask students if they can tell what most of the words have in common. Ask children what the *-ed* ending stands for. Challenge students to use each word in a sentence. Then invite them to use the words in a class story. As children suggest sentences with the vocabulary words, write them on chart paper. Read aloud the class story, underlining all the words that end in *-ed*. Students might discover that they've added other *-ed* words, too.

Discussion Questions

Discuss these questions *before* you read the book with students:

◆ Do children think their school is wheelchair accessible? Take the class for a walk around the school to look for places that might be difficult for a wheelchair-bound student to enter or move about. Consider common areas like the library, auditorium, or cafeteria.

Discuss these questions *while* you read the book with students:

◆ What does Arnie say to Philip that isn't very nice? How does he tease Philip?

◆ How do you feel about Arnie? How do you feel about Philip?

◆ How did Arnie change after his accident? What did he and Philip now have in common? What activities did they enjoy together?

Discuss these questions *after* you read the book with students:

◆ Did Arnie learn a lesson from his accident? If so, what was it?

◆ How can teachers and students include special-needs children in the daily routine? What more can be done at school?

◆ What should you do if you hear someone teasing another student? How do you feel when you are the one being teased? Discuss how mean words can hurt people's feelings.

Extension Activities

Sharing/Oral Language: Remind students that Philip shared his baseball card collection with Arnie. What would the children like to share with their classmates? Invite students to bring their hobbies and collections to school. Set aside time for a "Collection Show and Tell." Then encourage children to display their collections for the class, explaining a bit about the collection and why they enjoy collecting.

Role Play/Feelings: Invite children to role-play Arnie and Philip. Assign different parts of the story to different groups, such as when Philip first arrives at school, Arnie and Philip's first meeting, Arnie's accident, and so on. As children act out their roles, suggest that they pay attention to their feelings. Do they think their feelings are similar to how Arnie, Philip, or another child might react?

Storytelling/Problem Solving: Ask students to write a sequel to the story titled *Arnie and Philip Play Ball*. Students can share their sequels with the class. Also, ask students how they would modify the rules and equipment to make it possible for wheelchair-bound students to play ball.

Real-life Experience/Class Visitor: Invite a professional from a local hospital or clinic to bring a wheelchair to class and demonstrate how it works. If possible, let children sit in the wheelchair and try to maneuver it. Tell children to pretend that they do not have the use of their legs, and that their arms are too busy to do anything but push the wheels. Do they find it easy or difficult? Are they able to steer? Have the class send a thank-you note to your demonstrator.

Home Connection

Encourage children to look around their homes to see if they are wheelchair accessible. What changes would have to be made? Have students draw a picture of an area in the home, showing how they could make it easier for a person in a wheelchair to get around.

Activity Sheets

Visiting a Friend
Skill Level: Easy
Have students draw pictures of themselves doing activities with friends.

Write a Letter
Skill Level: Difficult
Have each student write a letter from Philip to one of his friends at his old school.

Name _____

Visiting a Friend

What do you do when you visit a friend? Draw a picture of yourself and a friend doing an activity together.

Reproducible

Name _____

Write a Letter

Philip was the new kid in school. He probably had friends at his old school.

What do you think Philip would tell his old friends about his new school?

Write a letter from Philip to one of his old friends.

Date _____

Dear _____ ,

Yesterday was the first day at my new school. _____

_____

_____

_____

_____

_____

_____

_____

_____

Your friend,

_____

Harry and Willy and Carrothead

by Judith Caseley
Publisher: Greenwillow Books, 1991
Type: Fiction

Book Summary

Three boys become friends and do all kinds of "regular" things together. Their story, written by Oscar (Carrothead), is about overcoming concerns about physical challenges and appearances.

Vocabulary

carriage	funnel	party	prosthesis
designs	neighbor	photograph	sword
fist	parrot	pirate	

Vocabulary Activity

Review the vocabulary words with the class. Point out that all the words can be used as nouns. Next, ask students to think of at least two adjectives to describe each vocabulary word. Then have children select five vocabulary words. Have them write a sentence for each of the five vocabulary words, using the two adjectives and the vocabulary word in the sentence.

Discussion Questions

Discuss these questions *before* you read the book with students:

◆ Look at the picture on the cover. What do you think this book might be about?

◆ What is a prosthesis? How do you think you should respond when you meet someone with a prosthesis? What would be a good thing to say or do?

Discuss these questions *while* you read the book with students:

◆ What does Harry do well? How did Harry compensate for the loss of his left hand?

◆ What does Harry's father mean when he says that Harry has "a mind of his own"? Is that a good characteristic for a child? Why do you think it was especially important for Harry to have a "mind of his own"?

◆ What is Oscar's nickname? Why is he called that? How does he feel about this name?

◆ Why do you think Harry was ready to fight for Oscar?

Discuss these questions *after* you read the book with students:

◆ How do you know that Harry is a "regular" kid? How did Harry's parents and his teacher help him to be "regular"?

◆ What do you imagine Harry might want to be when he grows up?

Extension Activities

Biography: Share a biography of Harry's hero, "Jim Abbott," by John Tolfe, in *Sports Illustrated*, 1991. Ask students to note what these two have in common.

Self-esteem/Writing: Encourage students to think about someone they admire. Who are their heroes? Ask each student to draw a picture of his or her hero. Explain that their heroes can be someone from their families, someone in the community, someone at school, or even someone who is famous. Suggest that children write a sentence or two about their heroes, explaining why they are special and why they admire them.

Vocabulary: Write the following words on the chalkboard: *snacktime, Carrothead, anything, airplane, playground, inside, fingernails,* and *scarecrow.* Ask students to figure out what these words from the book have in common. Review that a compound word is made up of two words. Have children divide each compound word into two words.

Self-esteem/Writing: What do children think it means to be a "regular" kid? Do children think they are regular kids? Invite students to write a short paragraph about themselves, describing the way they are "regular" kids. Then have them write a short paragraph about why they are "special." Encourage children to illustrate their paragraphs.

Role Play: Ask students to imagine that Willy and Oscar are older. They go to a baseball game. Who do they see playing baseball, but Harry! Have children role-play being Harry, Willy, and Oscar as adults, talking to Harry about his success on the baseball field.

Home Connection

Have students ask their parents to tell them stories about when they were toddlers. What is something funny they did? Encourage students to draw pictures and write a few sentences about the events. Invite volunteers to share their stories with the class.

Activity Sheets

Things to Do

Skill Level: Moderate

Have students list the things they do every day. Then encourage them to consider whether these things would be easy or difficult for Harry.

A Story of Friends

Skill Level: Difficult

Have students imagine that they are friends with Willy, Harry, or Oscar. Invite them to write a story about their friendship.

Name _____

Things to Do

Make a list of things that you do every day. Would these things be easy or hard for Harry to do? Draw a check mark under **Easy** or **Hard** to show what you think.

Things I Do	Easy	Hard
1.		
2.		
3.		
4.		
5.		
6.		
7.		

Name _____

A Story of Friends

Imagine that Harry, Willy, or Oscar is your friend. Write a story about your friendship.

_____ is my friend. We're just like "regular" kids. We

_____

_____

_____

_____

_____

_____

Draw a picture of yourself and your new friend.

What Do You Mean I Have a Learning Disability?

by Kathleen M. Dwyer
Publisher: Walker and Company, 1991
Type: Nonfiction

Book Summary

No one is sure why Jimmy is having trouble in school until he is identified as having a learning disability. The book explains the most common characteristics of a learning-disabled student and suggests some means of remediation. Jimmy becomes a happier child and a more successful student with help from his family and a tutor.

Vocabulary

attention	embarrassed	reverse	syllable
avoid	errors	sessions	tutor
conference	perception	stomach	visual

Vocabulary Activity

Discuss the meanings of the words with students. Then provide individual letter cards. If possible, use two different colors—one for consonants and one for vowels. Have students put the letters in order to spell each vocabulary word. For follow-up activities, challenge children to count the letters or syllables in each word.

Discussion Questions

Discuss these questions *before* you read the book with students:

- ◆ Look at the pictures of Jimmy in school and at home. What do you think this book might be about?

Discuss these questions *while* you read the book with students:

- ◆ In what ways is Jimmy like all other children?
- ◆ Why is Tom's friendship especially important to Jimmy? Why does it help to have a best friend when you are having problems at home or school?
- ◆ Who is Dr. Stone? Mrs. Sanchez? What is their relationship to Jimmy?
- ◆ How do Jimmy's parents and teachers help him?
- ◆ How does Jimmy feel when his grades improve? How does his family let him know they are proud of his hard work?

Discuss these questions *after* you read the book with students:

- ◆ What character traits does Jimmy have that make him successful in spite of his special needs?
- ◆ What should you do besides studying to prepare for a test?
- ◆ In what way do you use organizational skills every day? How do these skills help you?
- ◆ How can you help a student like Jimmy have a good experience at school?

Extension Activities

Graphing: Review what a character web is with children. Draw a blank character web on the chalkboard. Explain that the center circle tells who the web is about. The other circles tell things about that character. Invite students to complete a character web for Jimmy. Encourage them to describe his appearance, abilities, behavior, and personality traits.

Real-life Skills: Remind students that it is helpful for everyone to be organized. Help children become more organized by providing assignment sheets for them to track their work. Show students how to write down when an assignment is due, and the tasks that need to be done to complete it. Encourage them to keep color-coded folders for each subject. Devise a system to eliminate lost supplies. Allot a specific time each week to clean out desks and lockers. Share your organizational techniques with students.

Patterns/Shape: Provide students with a supply of assorted shapes that they can organize into patterns or tangrams to make pictures.

Spelling/Math: Prepare a container of individual letter cards. Invite children to use the cards for spelling practice. Have students work with partners. Each partner selects a specific number of letters, then spells any possible word using only those letters. Encourage them to set up a scoring system, for example, vowels equal one point, and consonants equal two points. The partner with the highest score wins the round.

Vocabulary/Grammar: Provide sets of word cards. Choose words that the class is currently studying. Place the word cards in your reading or spelling center. Challenge students to organize the words into complete sentences.

Math: Use plastic cubes or other manipulatives to reinforce math skills. Have students work in groups to write original word problems. Then ask them to challenge their classmates to figure out the word problems by showing answers with the correct manipulatives.

Cooperative Learning: Suggest a cooperative learning project. After dividing the class into groups of four to five students, help group members decide on tasks that rely on each group member's strength. For example, one child might excel at drawing, another at writing, another at speaking in front of the class, another at organizing, and another at constructing an art project. As children work together, have them notice how each member's special skill brings something important to the project.

Home Connection

Encourage students to write a paragraph that explains how Jimmy's feelings change throughout the story. How does Jimmy feel at the beginning? How does he feel at the end? Invite students to draw pictures that show Jimmy's progress. Students can read their paragraphs to their parents and talk about the book they have been working on at school.

Activity Sheets

Be the Teacher
Skill Level: Moderate
Have students use this activity sheet to correct spelling, math, and punctuation errors.

Jimmy's Secrets
Skill Level: Difficult
Have students write about the secrets Jimmy might tell his cat.

Name _____

Be the Teacher

Pretend you are Jimmy's teacher, and check his work. If the answer is correct, write a plus sign on the line. If the answer is incorrect, write the correct answer on the line.

Subtraction

1. 4 – 3 = 7 _____

2. 7 – 6 = 1 _____

3. 8 – 3 = 4 _____

4. 5 – 2 = 7 _____

5. 6 – 2 = 4 _____

6. 8 – 5 = 3 _____

7. 9 – 7 = 3 _____

Addition

1. 2 + 2 = 6 _____

2. 3 + 1 = 4 _____

3. 4 + 3 = 5 _____

4. 4 + 4 = 8 _____

5. 5 + 2 = 6 _____

6. 3 + 5 = 8 _____

7. 6 + 1 = 5 _____

Punctuate each sentence correctly and circle letters that should be capitalized. Then spell each color word.

Punctuation

1. i like pizza and hamburgers,

2. When is it time to go home.

3. dont be late for school!

4. Everyone will go on the trip.

5. can you help me find my books?

Spelling

1. pinck _____

2. blooe _____

3. grean _____

4. blake _____

5. purpal _____

Name _____

Jimmy's Secrets

1. Jimmy likes to tell secrets to his cat, Ebenezer. What is a secret?

    _____

    _____

    _____

2. What did Jimmy tell his cat?

    _____

    _____

    _____

3. What secret might Jimmy tell the cat about Dr. Stone?

    _____

    _____

    _____

4. What secret might Jimmy tell the cat about Mrs. Sanchez?

    _____

    _____

    _____

5. What secret might Jimmy tell the cat about his brothers?

    _____

    _____

     © Fearon Teacher Aids FE10001

What Do You Mean
I Have Attention Deficit Disorder?

by Kathleen M. Dwyer
Publisher: Walker and Company, 1996
Type: Nonfiction

Book Summary

Patrick has trouble with his behavior at home and at school. He can't concentrate on assignments, and he often misplaces things. After he is diagnosed with Attention Deficit Disorder, Patrick gets help from medical and school professionals and his family. The help he receives greatly improves his attitude and his academic performance.

Vocabulary

achievement	concentration	impulsive	pediatrician
appointment	curiosity	ingenious	pranks
attention	deficit	instructions	psychologist
complicate	evaluated	lecture	stamina

Vocabulary Activity

Many of the vocabulary words will be new to students. To help students learn the words, read the sentences from the book using the words, then substitute other words with similar meanings. Print or write the words on the chalkboard for students to see.

Discussion Questions

Discuss these questions *before* you read the book with students:

◆ Look at the pictures of Patrick in school. What do you think this book might be about?

◆ What do you think Attention Deficit Disorder is?

Discuss these questions *while* you read the book with students:

- Why do you think Patrick didn't like school?
- What did Patrick think about when his mind wandered?
- What did Miss Hogan, Dr. Lennon, and Patrick's parents do to help Patrick improve?
- How were Patrick's books and folders color-coded and numbered? How did this help Patrick?

Discuss these questions *after* you read the book with students:

- How did Patrick's behavior and school work improve?
- What are some ways to help people with Attention Deficit Disorder?
- Have you ever had a "terrible Tuesday"? What happened? Describe your day. How could you improve a "terrible Tuesday"?
- Do you have any study techniques that help you stay organized? Explain.

Extension Activities

Writing/Problem Solving: Encourage students to write about their own "terrible Tuesdays". Depending on the level of your class, have students write a paragraph or two describing the day. Combine students' work into a "Terrible Tuesdays" class book. Invite volunteers to read their paragraphs aloud, eliciting advice from their classmates on how they could have improved the day.

Listening/Following Directions: To hone listening and focusing skills, instruct students to listen closely as you give directions for drawing this picture:

Draw an oval in the center of your paper. On the left side of the oval near the top, draw a small rectangle pointing up toward the left corner of the page. Draw a small circle on the top of the rectangle. Add a V at the left edge of the small circle with the point of the V going away from the circle. At the right side of the oval, draw a long, thin triangle with the point touching the oval's side. Make two straight lines down from the center bottom of the oval. Add three short lines on the bottom of each of those lines.

Challenge students to tell you what they have drawn and its meaning in the story. The picture is a bird. Patrick's thoughts drifted off during class as he thought of the birds and other beautiful creatures of the marsh near his home. Patrick often drew pictures in his notebook instead of listening to the teacher.

Writing: To obtain more information about Attention Deficit Disorder, write a letter with your class to:

> Children and Adults with Attention Deficit Disorder
> 8181 Professional Place, Suite 201
> Landover, MD 20785

Share the response with the class.

Home Connection

Have students write short paragraphs or draw pictures of the chores they are expected to do at home. Encourage them to explain how they remember their chores. Are they rewarded for their chores? In what ways?

Activity Sheets

Take-Home Checklist

Make copies of the take-home checklist for students. Review the items listed down the left side of the page, as well as the days written across the top. Set aside a few minutes toward the end of each day for students to refer to the checklist, marking the school books they need to take home. Have students use the checklist for a specific period of time.

Getting Ready for School

Skill Level: Easy

Have students help Patrick get ready for school by indicating which items he needs to put in his book bag and which items he should wear.

Name _____

Take-Home Checklist

Keep this list at your desk during school. Check off the things you will need to take home each afternoon.

	Monday	Tuesday	Wednesday	Thursday	Friday
Reading book					
Reading workbook					
Library book					
Language arts homework					
Spelling book/homework					
Math book/homework					
Health book/homework					
Science book/homework					
Social Studies book/homework					
Other _____					
Assignment Sheet					

Name _____

Getting Ready for School

Help Patrick get ready for school. Draw arrows from the correct items to the book bag to show what goes inside it. Then draw arrows from the correct items to Patrick to show what he will wear.

Reproducible

Helping Hands

by Suzanne Haldane
Publisher: Dutton Children's Books, 1991
Type: Nonfiction

Book Summary

This book documents the training of a capuchin monkey, Willie, to help a quadriplegic teenager. Willie's assistance gives Greg a measure of independence, and her clever antics keep him occupied and entertained. They become fast friends.

Vocabulary

capuchin	independent	paralysis	reinforce
companion	instinct	quadriplegia	technique
cubicle	laser	quadriplegic	temperament
enable	midair	rehabilitation	vivid
flexible	pace		

Vocabulary Activity

Many of the vocabulary words may be difficult for students. To help them understand the meanings of the words, read the sentences from the book containing these words. Have students use context clues to figure out the meanings. Also ask students to substitute other words with similar meanings. Write the vocabulary words on the chalkboard. Then write sentences with a blank for students to fill in. For example, you might write: *A _____ cannot move his or her arms or legs.*

Discussion Questions

Discuss these questions *before* you read the book with students:

- ◆ What do you know about wheelchairs? Have you ever seen one? Do you know someone who uses one?

- ◆ Where do we usually see monkeys?

- ◆ What other animals help people with special needs?

Discuss these questions *while* you read the book with students:

- ◆ How did Greg become disabled?

- ◆ How does Greg operate his wheelchair? his computer? his telephone?

- ◆ Why were capuchin monkeys chosen to help quadriplegics?

- ◆ What characteristics of capuchin monkeys make them well-suited for helping quadriplegics?

- ◆ How do foster families help young monkeys become accustomed to human contact?

Discuss these questions *after* you read the book with students:

- ◆ Why has Willie become an important friend to Greg?

- ◆ What do you think about monkeys helping quadriplegics?

- ◆ Is a capuchin monkey a pet you would like to have? Why or why not?

Extension Activities

Sorting/Drawing Conclusions: Draw a two-column chart on the chalkboard. Ask students to list the things Willie can do for Greg in one column and the things he cannot do for Greg in the other column. Examine the results and ask students to draw conclusions about the things Willie can and cannot do.

Letter Writing: Encourage students to find out more about the Helping Hands program by writing to:

HELPING HANDS
1505 Commonwealth Avenue
Boston, MA 02135

Creative Writing: Ask students to consider how Greg's Doberman pinscher, Trapper, got along with Willie. How do they imagine Trapper might have felt when Willie was first introduced into Greg's home? Ask students to show the relationship between the two animals by drawing comic strips. Have students divide a sheet of paper into four parts. In each section, ask them to draw Willie and Trapper with speech bubbles above their heads. Then instruct students to write what Trapper and Willie say to each other in the speech bubbles.

Community Connection

Contact the Easter Seals organization in your community. Ask them about the services they provide for people with special needs. Do they refer individuals to programs for animal assistants? Do they provide adaptive devices for computers? Invite a representative from Easter Seals or health professional to your class to explain common spinal cord injuries and the resulting health problems.

Activity Sheets

A Capuchin Monkey at Work: Make a Mini-Book
Skill Level: Easy
Have students draw the pictures and then cut them apart to make mini-books. Covers for their mini-books can be made from separate sheets of paper.

Capuchin Monkeys in the Wild
Skill Level: Difficult
Have students use this activity sheet as they research information about capuchin monkeys in the wild. Review the questions with students and suggest resources they can use. Invite students to report their findings to the class.

Name _____

A Capuchin Monkey at Work: Make a Mini-Book

Draw a picture for each caption. Cut the pictures apart. Make a cover for your mini-book from a separate sheet of paper. Staple the pages together.

The monkey prepares a drink.

The monkey helps with the mouthstick.

The monkey plays a tape.

The monkey arranges a book.

Reproducible

Name _____

Capuchin Monkeys in the Wild

Research information about capuchin monkeys to answer the questions below. Write your answers in complete sentences.

1. In which countries do they live?_____

_____

2. Describe their appearance and size. _____

_____

3. What do they eat? _____

_____

4. Describe their habitat. _____

_____

5. Describe their family structure._____

_____

6. How are capuchins different from larger monkeys? _____

_____

Draw a picture of a capuchin monkey below.

Silent Lotus

by Jeanne M. Lee
Publisher: Farrar, Straus, Giroux, 1991
Type: Fiction

Book Summary

A young Cambodian girl, born deaf, dances so beautifully that she is welcomed into the king's court ballet.

Vocabulary

canals	egret	imitated	misfortune
cherished	gesture	jasmine	pavilion
crane	heron	lotus	vibrations

Vocabulary Activity

Review the vocabulary words with the class. Encourage students to use the words in sentences. Students can also find each word in the book and read the sentence aloud in which it appears. Help them figure out the meaning of each word using the illustrations or the prompts found in the text.

Make copies of the manual alphabet (Appendix A, page 106), and distribute them to students. Slowly spell a word from the vocabulary list and ask students to identify the word you are spelling. Invite them to practice spelling words for you to "read" in this way, too.

Discussion Questions

Discuss these questions *before* you read the book with students:

◆ Look at the pictures in the book. Describe the climate and the setting. What conclusions can you draw about the climate and setting of this story?

Discuss these questions *while* you read the book with students:

◆ Why can't Lotus speak? How are hearing and speaking connected?

◆ Why did the children refuse to play with Lotus? How do you feel when you are left out of something your classmates are doing?

◆ How do you think Lotus felt when she saw the city gates?

◆ Why was Lotus well accepted by the court dancers?

◆ How does Lotus express her emotions? Give examples from the story.

Discuss these questions *after* you read the book with students:

◆ How do you feel at the end of the story? How do you feel toward Lotus?

◆ How might Lotus's life have been different if she had a brother or sister?

◆ How do you think you and your teacher could help a hearing-impaired student?

Extension Activities

Geography: Help students locate Cambodia on a world map. Have them note the countries that surround Cambodia. Ask them to point out the Gulf of Thailand and the capital city. Challenge students to figure out the vast distance between Cambodia and the United States, measuring across the Pacific Ocean. Have students research information about the Angkor Wat Temple.

Social Studies: Ask children to look at the pictures of the houses in the book. Have them describe how the houses are different from houses they usually see. Encourage students to draw conclusions about why these types of houses are built. Ask them where else houses like this might be built.

Science/Art: Ask students to note illustrations of birds in the book. Have them note what the egrets, herons, and cranes have in common. Ask students to think about how the birds' long legs help them. Then have students draw pictures of the three birds on thin cardboard. Students can cut out the birds and tape on wooden chopsticks for legs. Have students stick their birds in clay bases for a bird display.

Science/Music: Share with students that Lotus can "experience" music because she can feel the vibrations that music makes. Let students explore several instruments, such as a triangle, a gong, or guitar. Have students closely observe a struck instrument as it vibrates back and forth. Ask students to place hands on the instrument to stop the vibration. The book, *The Science of Music* by Melvin Berger (Thomas Crowell Junior Books, 1989), is an excellent resource for this activity.

Large-Motor Skills/Cooperative Learning: Have students work with partners or in small groups to tell stories using only hand and body gestures. Suggest that they choose a common folktale or fairy tale. Set aside time for students to rehearse, then invite groups to share their silent stories.

Activity Sheets

Lots About Lotus

Skill Level: Moderate

Have students use their knowledge about Lotus to complete the sentences. Invite them to draw pictures of Lotus at home and at the temple.

Story Web

Skill Level: Difficult

Have students complete a story web by writing or drawing something about the setting, characters, problem, and solution of the story.

Name _____

Lots About Lotus

You learned all about Lotus. Share what you know by completing each sentence. The words in the box will help you.

lake	friends	stars	happy
hear	moon	dancers	temple

1. Lotus and her family lived in a house by a _____ .

2. Lotus's face was round as the _____ .

3. Lotus's eyes were bright as the _____ .

4. Lotus could not _____ or speak.

5. Her parents took her to the _____ in the city.

6. Lotus liked to see the court _____ .

7. Lotus made many _____ living at the court.

8. She was _____ dancing for the King and Queen.

Draw a picture of Lotus at home.

Draw Lotus dancing for the King.

Name _____

Story Web

Complete a web for the story *Silent Lotus* by writing or drawing something about the setting, characters, problem, and solution of the story.

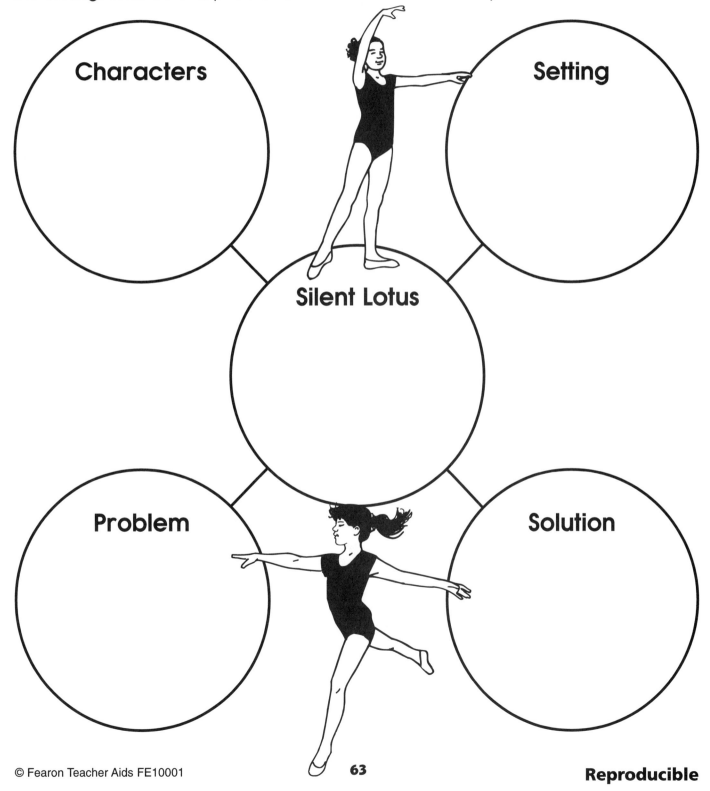

Reproducible

Knots on a Counting Rope

by Bill Martin Jr. and John Archambault
Publisher: Henry Holt and Company, 1997
Type: Fiction

Book Summary

A blind Indian boy asks his grandfather to retell the story of his birth. Despite his disability, the boy is able to train and race a horse. This classic book gives insight into Native American culture, the relationship between a child and his grandfather, and the overcoming of a disability.

Vocabulary

canyon	foal	knots	shallow
ceremony	frail	rainbow	tribal
colt	hogan	reins	

Vocabulary Activity

Review the meanings of the vocabulary words with students. Then give each child a copy of the Braille alphabet (Appendix B, page 107). Explain to children that the dots are actually raised so that a blind person can feel them. Use the Braille letters to write a word from the vocabulary list on the chalkboard. Ask students to identify the word. Invite students to write several words using the Braille letters.

Discussion Questions

Discuss these questions *before* you read the book with students:

- ◆ Do you know anyone who is vision-impaired? What daily living tasks are difficult for them? How can you help them?

- ◆ What activities do you enjoy doing with your grandfather or an older relative?

- ◆ Have you ever ridden a horse? What did you like or dislike about riding it?

Discuss these questions *while* you read the book with students:

- ◆ What do the blue horses symbolize?

- ◆ Why was Rainbow important to Boy?

- ◆ How did Boy react when he did not win the race?

Discuss these questions *after* you read the book with students:

- ◆ Describe Boy's relationship with Grandfather. What is your relationship like with your grandparents?

- ◆ How did Boy work to overcome his special needs?

- ◆ How do you feel when you try hard but do not win?

- ◆ What makes you feel especially strong?

- ◆ How will Boy adjust to life without Grandfather?

Extension Activities

Self-esteem/Art: Recall with students how Boy's name, "Boy-Strength-of-Blue-Horses," reflects nature. Invite students to come up with "nature" names for themselves. Invite them to draw pictures that represent their names, perhaps adding a sentence about why these names are appropriate for them. Students can also make sand paintings of their names. Before class, mix powdered tempera with sand in small lidded jars. Cut tan construction paper into 6" (15-cm) square pieces. Students can then draw their designs on the paper, go over the designs with white glue, and sprinkle on colored sand.

Oral Language/Research: Invite students to research several topics related to blindness, including:

- some causes of blindness

- what some blind people must do each day to adjust to the lack of vision

- how Louis Braille developed the Braille alphabet

Students can discuss their findings with the class.

Class Visitor/Letter Writing: Invite a resource person, such as a teacher of the blind or a blind person, to speak with your class. Ask your visitor to focus the discussion on how students should interact with a blind person. Have the class write a thank-you note to your guest, thanking them for their time.

Community Connection

Ask students to check for Braille signs in their community. Where do students see Braille signs? What are the signs used for? Where else would Braille signs be useful? Ask students to report their findings to the class.

Activity Sheets

Braille Alphabet (Appendix B, page 107)
Students use this resource for the vocabulary activity.

Break the Code
Skill Level: Easy
Have students read the Braille letters on this activity sheet to figure out the name of the horse.

What Is a Color?
Skill Level: Moderate
Have students complete sentences to explain the colors *yellow* and *green*.

Name _____

Break the Code

The horse's name is written below, it is written using the Braille alphabet. Break the code! Write the letters for the Braille symbols on the lines to show the horse's name. Color the page when you are finished.

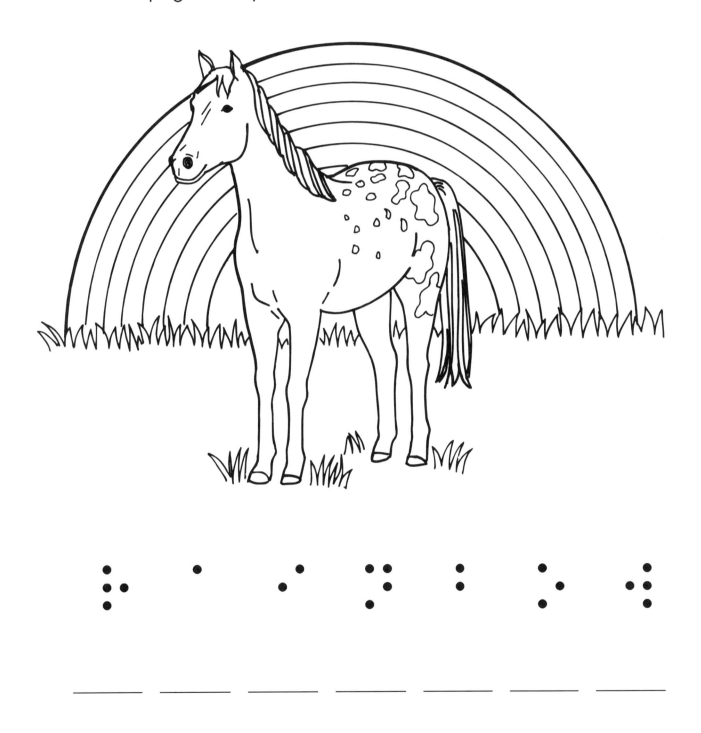

_____ _____ _____ _____ _____ _____ _____

Name _____

What Is a Color?

To help Boy understand blue, Grandfather told him that blue was *the morning, the sunrise, the sky, the song of the birds,* and *the feeling of a spring day beginning.*

How would you explain yellow and green to Boy? Complete each sentence below with several words that explain these colors.

Yellow is _____

_____

_____

_____

_____

Green is _____

_____

_____

_____

_____

Describe a color of your choice below.

_____ is _____

_____

_____

_____

_____

Summer Tunes:
A Martha's Vineyard Vacation

by Patricia McMahon
Publisher: Boyds Mills Press, 1996
Type: Nonfiction

Book Summary

Ten-year-old Conor Healy, born with cerebral palsy, enjoys a family vacation on Martha's Vineyard. The highlight of the trip for Conor is a visit to radio station WMVY's disc jockey, Barbara Dacey. Conor loves music, and he hopes to become a DJ someday.

Vocabulary

caravan	elevator	helm	profusion
clamors	ferry	island	shrivel
despicable	frustration	monitor	wake
destination	grimaces	podium	

Vocabulary Activity

Write the vocabulary words on the chalkboard. Talk about the meanings of the words as they are used in the story. Assign groups of words to student pairs. Have students think of sentences for their assigned words. Encourage students to share their sentences with the class.

Discussion Questions

Discuss these questions *before* you read the book with students:

   ◆ Show students the photos in the book. Who are the members of the Healy family? Who is Hershey?

Discuss these questions *while* you read the book with students:

◆ How did Martha's Vineyard get its name?

◆ Which activities does the family enjoy doing together? How is Conor included? How do these activities compare to the things your family likes to do?

◆ What does Conor like more than anything else?

◆ What is the meaning of the name of the family boat, *Canora*?

◆ Where on the island is it impossible for Conor to go? What should be changed to make these places more accessible?

Discuss these questions *after* you read the book with students:

◆ How do the Healys accommodate Conor's special needs on their boat, on bikes, at the beach, and in their family vacation home?

◆ How does Conor react to Mrs. Nasty Despicable and the lady with the ice-cream money? Explain his feelings in detail. How do *you* feel about the situation?

Extension Activities

Geography/Map Skills: Challenge students to locate Martha's Vineyard and Cape Cod on a map of the United States. Help them estimate the distance from the Healy's vacation home to the students' hometowns. If students were driving from Martha's Vineyard to their hometowns, through which states would they pass?

Creative Writing: Ask children to imagine that Conor is a student in their class, and consider these issues: How would the classroom need to be changed to meet Conor's needs? How would Conor interact with teachers and students? Remind students that Conor would probably need his wheelchair to get around. Is the school wheelchair-accessible? Then have students write short stories describing a typical school day for Conor. Invite children to read their stories for the class.

Role Play/Community Awareness: Invite volunteers to role-play the scene between Conor, his mother, and Mrs. Nasty Despicable. Conclude by explaining the law regarding handicapped parking in your community.

Music/Language: Have students work in groups to come up with short songs about the Healy's family vacation. Create an original melody or use the melody of a familiar song, such as "London Bridge Is Falling Down." Have students change the words to reflect the family vacation. Encourage students to share their songs with the class, or let groups record songs on a tape recorder to play again.

Research: Encourage students to find out more about cerebral palsy. What causes the condition? How is it treated? How many people in the United States are affected by cerebral palsy? Discuss the explanation for Conor's condition.

Home Connection

Ask students to write a story about their families' most recent vacations or something enjoyable they recently did with their families. Have children bring in photographs to share with the class.

Activity Sheets

Our Photo Albums

Skill Level: Easy

Have students draw a picture of Conor's vacation and a picture of their own vacation.

Alike and Different

Skill Level: Moderate

Have students look at their pictures from the activity on page 72. Invite students to write about how their vacations were alike and different from Conor's vacation.

Ice-Cream Time

Skill Level: Moderate

Have students calculate the total price of a treat for the family.

Name _____

Our Photo Albums

Draw a picture of Conor's vacation.

Conor's Photo Album

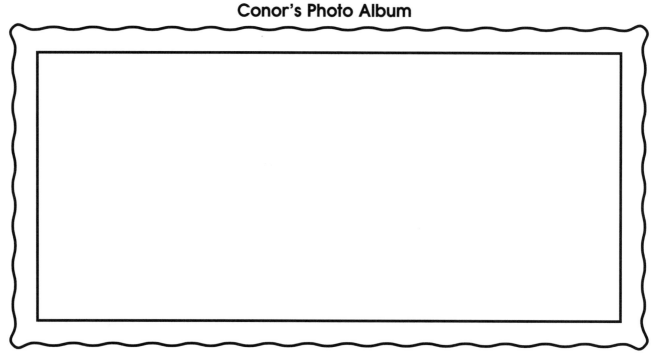

Draw a picture of your vacation.

_____ **Photo Album**

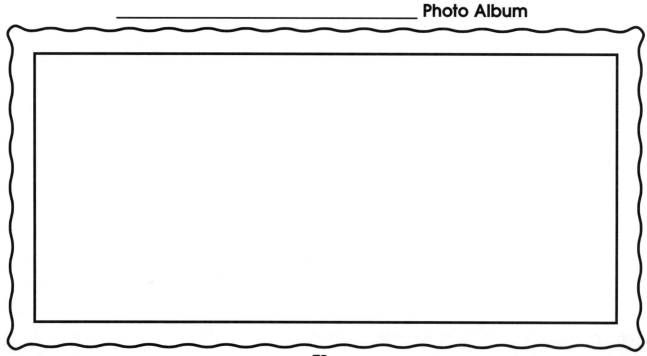

Name _____

Alike and Different

How was your vacation like Conor's vacation?

_____

_____

_____

_____

_____

_____

_____

How was your vacation different from Conor's vacation?

_____

_____

_____

_____

_____

_____

_____

Name _____

Ice-Cream Time

Choose a treat from the menu for each family member. Write the name of the treat and the price for each person. Then add up all the prices to come up with the total bill.

Cool Treats

chocolate	vanilla	strawberry
butter pecan	peppermint	chocolate chip
orange sherbet	raspberry yogurt	

One-dip cone	$1.00	Two-dip cone	$1.75
Small sundae	$1.35	Large sundae	$2.50
Ice-cream bar	$ .75	Large cookie	$ .99

	Order	Prices
Tom Healy	_____	_____
Joan Healy	_____	_____
Carrie Healy	_____	_____
Brenna Healy	_____	_____
Conor Healy	_____	_____
	Total	_____

Imagine Me on a Sit-Ski!

by George Moran
Publisher: Albert Whitman & Company, 1994
Type: Fiction

Book Summary

A boy with cerebral palsy overcomes not only his physical challenge, but also his fears when he joins his classmates on a ski trip.

Vocabulary

accessible	equipment	lodge	snowmobile
adaptive	experts	padding	tether
chairlift	helmet	sit-ski	van
challenged	kayak	slopes	wordboard

Vocabulary Activity

Create a wordboard or use a set of letter tiles. List the vocabulary words on the chalkboard. Invite students to come to the wordboard to spell each word. Talk about the meanings of the words, and ask students to use the words in sentences.

Discussion Questions

Discuss these questions *before* you read the book with students:

- Have you ever been on an overnight trip with friends or classmates? Tell about your experiences.

- What special considerations should group leaders make when planning a ski trip for physically challenged individuals?

Discuss these questions *while* you read the book with students:

◆ How would you describe Mr. Johnson and Ms. Harris? How did the students feel about their teachers?

◆ What changes were made to make the ski lodge wheelchair accessible?

◆ What adaptive equipment did the class use?

◆ How did Billy control his sit-ski? How did the instructors protect him?

◆ What were the children able to do together, other than ski?

Discuss these questions *after* you read the book with students:

◆ What did Billy learn about himself from his ski experiences?

◆ What new sports is Billy looking forward to trying because of the confidence he gained on the ski trip?

◆ How do you imagine it feels to ride in a sit-ski? Would you like to give it a try?

◆ If you have ever gone skiing, explain how Billy's experience was similar or different from yours.

◆ What would you think if you saw someone riding on a sit-ski?

Extension Activities

Writing/Real-life Experience: Instruct students to create wordboards similar to the one Billy uses. Have students use the wordboards to send messages to their friends. Encourage students to talk about the experience. How does it affect their ability to communicate? What would it be like to have thoughts but no ability to speak? Invite students to try the wordboards using unsharpened pencils as pointers.

Writing: Share with children that teachers often keep journals of special events they participate in with their classes. Ask students what the teachers in this story might write about the trip and Billy's participation. Encourage students to write journal entries for them. Ask them to talk about the preparation the teachers made for the trip and how they feel after Billy successfully manages the sit-ski. Combine students' journal entries into a class journal.

Sequencing: Have students write about or draw pictures of things that happen in the story on separate cards. Mix the cards together and give them to a volunteer. Challenge him or her to put the cards in story order.

Math: Have younger students review the text and write a schedule for the ski trip. Then ask students to show you the times by moving the hands on a manipulative clock.

Role Play: Divide the class into groups to role-play scenes from the story. Review with them Billy's initial fear, culminating in his final enjoyment of the skiing apparatus. Students might also role-play a scene at Billy's home with his parents after the ski trip. Make sure all group members participate as they react to Billy's story.

Community Connection

Set up a field trip to visit a sports facility in your area. You could also check out roller rinks, miniature golf courses, local parks, lakes with boat rentals, or other facilities common in your area. Challenge students to notice the accommodations that have been made for the physically challenged, if any. You might write ahead, asking an official to give your class a tour to point out how the area is accessible to the physically challenged. Afterward, help students write a note to thank the official for the tour.

Activity Sheet

What You Need on a Sit-Ski

Skill Level: Easy

Have students examine the equipment needed to safely use a sit-ski.

Name _____

What You Need on a Sit-Ski

Billy is getting ready to ride on the sit-ski. What does Billy need? Draw items on Billy. (Hint: The things Billy needs are next to him.)

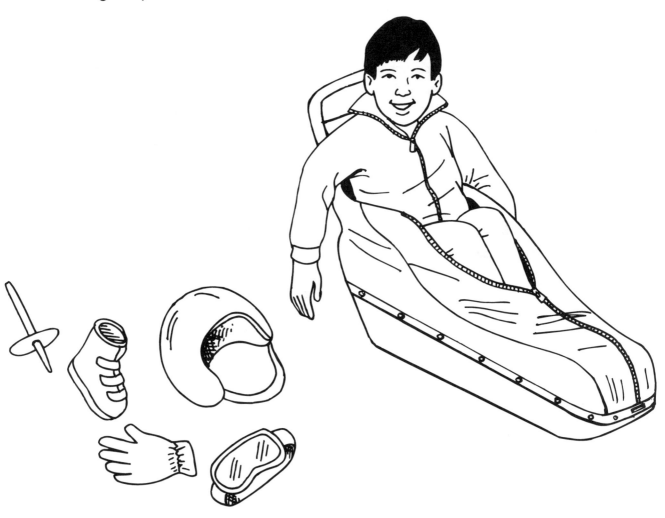

Choose one of the things Billy needs. Explain why this item is important below.

_____

_____

_____

_____

_____

Beethoven Lives Upstairs

by Barbara Nichol
Publisher: Orchard Books, 1994
Type: Fiction

Book Summary

Set in Vienna (1822–25), this story is the compilation of letters written by a young boy, Christoph, to his uncle about an eccentric boarder living in his home. The boarder is none other than the composer Ludwig van Beethoven, a man isolated from mainstream society by his deafness and his musical genius.

Vocabulary

aid	innocent	orchestra	symphony
composer	inquiries	peculiar	tidy
conductor	laughingstock	procession	tread
console	metronome	respects	uproar
incident	nimble	soprano	vanished

Vocabulary Activity

Review the meanings of the vocabulary words used in the story. Then encourage students to spell the words using the manual alphabet (Appendix A, page 106).

Remind students that people used a notebook to communicate in writing with Beethoven because he could not hear. Ask students to write five questions using the vocabulary words. Have them exchange papers with classmates and write answers to the questions.

Discussion Questions

Discuss these questions *before* you read the book with students:

◆ Who is Ludwig van Beethoven? Why is he famous?

Discuss these questions *while* you read the book with students:

◆ How does Christoph feel about Beethoven at the beginning of the book?

◆ What does Beethoven do to make Christoph believe he is a madman?

◆ Where is Christoph's father?

◆ How does Christoph's mother feel about Beethoven?

◆ Describe Beethoven's appearance.

◆ What special need does Beethoven have in addition to his deafness? Explain what he does to rest after a hard day's work.

Discuss these questions *after* you read the book with students:

◆ What is the relationship between Christoph and Beethoven by the end of the book? How and why has it changed?

◆ Explain Beethoven's "restless nature." How does his special need contribute to his restlessness?

◆ How would your life change if a man like Beethoven lived upstairs?

◆ How would Beethoven's life have been different if he had lived in modern times?

◆ Which musician or singer of today would you like to have living above you? Why?

Extension Activities

Literature Connection/History: Share the book *Introducing Beethoven* by Roland Vernon (Silver Burdett, 1996). It provides factual information about the composer and his work. Students can then create a class time line to show the events of Beethoven's life and musical career. Challenge students to find out what was going on in the United States during that same time period.

Geography/Map Skills: Recall with students that this story takes place in Europe. Ask a student to locate Europe on a wall map. Which ocean lies between the United States and Europe? Encourage students to find Germany and Austria. Would they say these countries are in the north, south, or central region of Europe? Finally, challenge students to find the cities of Vienna and Salzburg in Austria and Bonn and Baden in Germany.

Music/Art: Play a recording for students of Beethoven's *Ninth Symphony*. What words or phrases does the symphony evoke for children as they listen to it? Write down their ideas. Students can draw pictures that show how they feel or what they think about as they listen to the symphony. Students can also listen to Beethoven's *Fifth Symphony* and complete similar activities.

Role Play/Writing: Assign pairs of students to role-play scenes between Beethoven and Christoph. The scenes can be based on an incident from the story or situations that partners make up. Have each pair work together to write a loose script for their scene. Then invite pairs to share their scenes with the class.

Video Connection/Writing: Obtain a copy of the video *Beethoven Lives Upstairs* (Classical Productions for Children Limited, Toronto, Ontario, BMG Distribution, 1992). The video is 52 minutes long. Have students compare the video to the story they read. How was the story the same? What, if anything, was different in the video? Ask students to write reviews of the video.

Home Connection

Encourage students to ask their parents if they like Beethoven's music. Which type of music, composer, singer, or performer are their parents' favorites? In class, record students' findings on a chart.

Activity Sheet

Neighborly Thoughts
Skill Level: Moderate
This activity sheet encourages students to put themselves in the shoes of Beethoven and Christoph. Encourage students to write what Beethoven and Christoph might be thinking about.

Name _____

Neighborly Thoughts

What might Beethoven be thinking? What might Christoph be thinking? Write what they are thinking on the lines.

Beethoven _____

_____

_____

_____

_____

_____

Christoph _____

_____

_____

_____

_____

_____

My Buddy

by Audrey Osofsky
Publisher: Henry Holt and Company, 1992
Type: Fiction

Book Summary

A golden retriever service dog is the best friend of the boy in this story. The boy has muscular dystrophy and must rely on the dog to help him with a variety of simple tasks. Because of the dog's assistance, the boy enjoys life with a new measure of independence.

Vocabulary

attention	fetch	muscles	service dog
command	focus	muscular dystrophy	training
disease	golden retriever	obey	

Vocabulary Activity

Discuss the meanings of the vocabulary words in the context of the story. Then print each word on a large index card. As you show each card to students, ask them to clap and count the syllables in the word. Conclude by having students print the words on paper. Instruct them to circle the vowels with a red crayon and underline the consonants with a blue crayon.

Discussion Questions

Discuss these questions *before* you read the book with students:

◆ What could you do to help a student with a special need?

◆ Do you think friends ever get tired of helping? Explain.

- How would you feel if there were a service dog in your classroom? What would be the same? How would things be different?

- How would you describe a friend? Do you think an animal can be a friend? Why or why not?

Discuss these questions *while* you read the book with students:

- Describe how Buddy looks and acts. What does he do to help the boy?

- Compare and contrast the boy's life before and after Buddy arrives.

Discuss these questions *after* you read the book with students:

- Why do you think the boy is never named in the story?

- How would your life change if you or your best friend were suddenly confined to a wheelchair?

- How would Buddy's life be different if he were a family pet rather than a service dog? Would Buddy go to school? What would Buddy do during the day?

Extension Activities

Creative Writing: Have students write a story about a day at school from Buddy's point of view. What does Buddy do for the boy in school at different times of the day? What is Buddy's favorite way to help the boy? What does Buddy think about the teacher and the other students?

Critical Thinking: Have students review the book for all the commands that Buddy learns. Write them on the chalkboard. Then have students brainstorm over several days a list of other commands Buddy might learn. Challenge students to come up with 60 commands.

Letter Writing: Ask children what else they would like to know about service dogs like Buddy. List their questions on the chalkboard or chart paper. Then compose a letter with the class and send it to:

Canine Companions for Independence
P.O. Box 446
Santa Rosa, California 95402

Share the response with the class.

Art/Writing: Talk with students about the things Buddy does for the boy. Also point out that the boy does lots of things for Buddy, such as feed him, brush him, and play ball with him. Have each student divide a sheet of white drawing paper in half. On one half, have them illustrate something that Buddy does for the boy. On the other half, ask them to illustrate something the boy does for Buddy. Encourage students to write captions for their pictures as well. Display the pictures on a bulletin board titled *Buddies Help Each Other*.

Home and Community Connection

Ask students to look for ways their neighborhood has prepared for wheelchair access on their way to and from school. Also, ask students what would need to be done to accommodate a wheelchair in their homes. Encourage children to draw a picture of a change they could make to their neighborhood or home to accommodate a wheelchair.

Activity Sheets

Buddy's Backpack
Skill Level: Moderate
Have students list and draw things in the boy's backpack when he goes to school and when he goes to his friend Mike's house.

Compound Words
Skill Level: Difficult
Have students review compound words used in the story.

Name _____

Buddy's Backpack

What things are in Buddy's backpack when the boy goes to school? Write these things on the lines. Draw pictures of them next to the backpack.

_____

_____

_____

_____

_____

_____

_____

What things are in Buddy's backpack when the boy goes to Mike's house? Write these things on the lines. Draw pictures of them next to the backpack.

_____

_____

_____

_____

_____

Name _____

Compound Words

The compound words below are all mixed up. Draw a line from each word in the left column to a word in the right column to make a compound word. Write the compound words on the lines.

lunch	side	_____
back	time	_____
wheel	bell	_____
base	shop	_____
barber	ball	_____
door	room	_____
out	chair	_____
bed	pack	_____

Choose four of the compound words. Use each one in a sentence.

1. _____

   _____

2. _____

   _____

3. _____

   _____

4. _____

   _____

Our Teacher's in a Wheelchair

by Mary Ellen Powers
Publisher: Albert Whitman & Company, 1986
Type: Nonfiction

Book Summary

A young man is confined to a wheelchair due to an injury sustained while playing college sports. The story demonstrates that he is able to have a happy personal life and a successful career as a teacher in a day-care center.

Vocabulary

bicycle	gravel	injury	paralyzed
college	handicapped	lacrosse	wheelchair
equipment	hospital	paralysis	

Vocabulary Activity

Define the vocabulary words and discuss how each word is important in the story. Ask students to use each word in a sentence that relates to the story. Then print the words on large index cards and cut apart the words into syllables. Mix up the cards and place them in a pile. Have students arrange the syllable cards into words.

Discussion Questions

Discuss these questions *before* you read the book with students:

- ◆ How would you feel about having a teacher who is confined to a wheelchair? List five ways it would change your school day.

Discuss these questions *while* you read the book with students:

◆ How are Brian's apartment and car adapted so he can live independently?

◆ Should the children be afraid of catching Brian's condition? Explain.

◆ What problems did Brian experience with his wheelchair?

Discuss these questions *after* you read the book with students:

◆ What other kinds of careers could Brian have chosen?

◆ Why is it important to ask people for help when you need it?

◆ How would being in a wheelchair change your life?

Extension Activities

Writing: How do students imagine Brian felt before his first day at the day-care center? If Brian wrote in a journal, how would he describe his feelings? Have students write journal entries for Brian. Encourage them to consider Brian's challenges and the responsibilities he will have at the center.

Observing/Writing: Let students check to see in what ways their school is wheelchair accessible. Have students list what accommodations have been made for chair-bound students or visitors. Then have students write paragraphs describing accommodations that could be made.

Real-life Experience: If possible, bring a folding wheelchair to class. Let students practice using it and folding it. Then discuss the experience with them.

Sorting: Draw a two-column chart on the chalkboard. Have students list things that Brian can do with his friends in one column and things that Brian cannot do in the other column.

Community Connection

Ask students to look around their neighborhood and community for wheelchair ramps and for businesses that provide handicapped parking. Have them report their findings to the class. Ask them to draw the handicapped parking symbol.

Activity Sheet

Yes, I Can!
Skill Level: Easy
Have students write about the things Brian can do.

Name _____

Yes, I Can!

On the lines below, write six things that Brian can do. Then color the picture.

1. _____

2. _____

3. _____

4. _____

5. _____

6. _____

90

The Balancing Girl

by Berniece Rabe
Publisher: Dutton, 1981
Type: Fiction

Book Summary

Margaret, a physically challenged first grader with exceptional fine motor skills, balances dominoes for her booth at the school carnival. She is very successful, earning $101.30 toward the purchase of new gym equipment.

Vocabulary

announced	booth	cylinder	spires
appointed	carnival	dominoes	upright
balance	crutches	guards	wheelchair

Vocabulary Activity

Go over the vocabulary words with the class. Assign several words to student pairs. Have students write sentences using the words. Invite them to share their sentences with the class.

Discussion Questions

Discuss these questions *before* you read the book with students:

◆ Have you ever been to a carnival? Did you win any prizes? What booth did you like the best? Why?

Discuss these questions *while* you read the book with students:

◆ Who do you think spoiled Margaret's castle? Why would this person do such a thing?

◆ Do you know anyone like Tommy? How do you think he made Margaret feel? What could he have done to get along with her?

◆ How can you tell that William is a good friend to Margaret?

◆ How do we know from the story that Margaret has adjusted well to her special need? Use examples from the story to explain your answer.

Discuss these questions *after* you read the book with students:

◆ What is your best skill? How can you use it to help others? How might it help you when you grow up? (Remind students that everyone, regardless of special needs, has something they can contribute to society. It is important to recognize and value individual strengths.)

◆ What kind of booth would you create for a school carnival?

◆ Suppose Tommy and Margaret work together on a booth for the next carnival. What might they plan?

◆ How could Ms. Joliet have helped the students become accustomed to Margaret?

◆ How could the other students help Margaret during the school day?

Extension Activities

Fine Motor Skills: Encourage students to try balancing dominoes the way Margaret does in the story with fancy curves, snaky S's, and little stairs. Do they find these tasks difficult or easy? What do they think about Margaret's special skills?

Math: Remind students that Margaret earned $101.30 at the school carnival. Have students use play money (bills and coins) to count up to $101.30. Invite small groups to work independently, then share their money combinations with the class. Write the combinations on the chalkboard, each time challenging the next group to come up with a new combination.

Research/Critical Thinking: The book does not state the cause of Margaret's condition. It is possible, however, that she has the spinal defect *spina bifida*. Ask students to find out more about spina bifida, including its causes and ways to manage the condition. Ask students what other conditions or accidents might cause a person to be confined to a wheelchair.

Home Connection

Remind students that even though Margaret has special needs, she also has a talent for balancing things. Ask students to describe some talents their family members have. Invite students to draw pictures of the people in their families, then write one sentence about each family member that describes his or her special talents.

Activity Sheet

At the School Carnival

Skill Level: Easy

Have students cut and paste the correct labels on the carnival booths.

Name _____

At the School Carnival

The students forgot to put the signs on the carnival booths! Help them out. Cut out the signs at the bottom of the page. Glue them to the correct booths.

✂ --

| **Ring Toss** | **Fish Pond** | **Clown** |

Alex Is My Friend

by Marisabina Russo
Publisher: Greenwillow Books, 1992
Type: Fiction

Book Summary

Ben and Alex are friends. They share soccer games, snacks, jokes, and birthday parties. Eventually Ben realizes that Alex is not growing and is told that his friend has a condition called "dwarfism." Their friendship remains strong while Alex recuperates from surgery for a back problem.

Vocabulary

alien	noises	sisters	stroller
dinosaur	operation	snacks	superheroes
hospital	scary	soccer	weird

Vocabulary Activity

Review the meaning of each vocabulary word. Then ask students to choose two words and write a sentence using both words. Have students suggest other pairs of words. Encourage students to make their sentences fun and silly. They can also write the words in alphabetical order.

Discussion Questions

Discuss these questions *before* you read the book with students:

◆ What activities do you share with your friends?

◆ Have you ever had surgery? What was it like to be in a hospital?

Discuss these questions *while* you read the book with students:

◆ How did Alex and Ben first meet? Who is Amy?

◆ How are Ben and Alex alike? How are they different?

◆ Why is a remote-control car or a kite a poor choice to give a child recovering from surgery?

◆ What present would you have given Alex after his operation?

◆ What gift would you wish to receive if you were recovering from surgery?

Discuss these questions *after* you read the book with students:

◆ What adaptations will Alex need to help him live as an independent adult? Consider how he will get around the community, cook for himself, keep a job, and so on.

◆ Might Ben stop growing because of his friendship with Alex?

Extension Activities

Role Play: Invite students to role-play story-related scenes. Some scenarios might include: the two girls talking about their brothers, Alex and Ben; Alex and Ben talking about their sisters; Alex and his sister talking about Ben and his sister, and vice versa. Suggest that the characters talk about relationships, problems, and family life. They might also discuss what their families do after soccer games.

Also have students role-play a telephone conversation between Alex and Ben after the surgery, but before Ben's visit. Alex might recount the hospital experience, and Ben could bring Alex up to date on events in the neighborhood and school. After a short rehearsal time, invite students to share their role plays with the class.

Writing: Recall with students that Alex loves a good joke. Invite the class to create a joke book with pages shaped like a big smile. Ask each student to write a favorite joke or riddle on a page for the book. Create a cover with the title *Alex's Joke Book*. Staple all the pages together. Each morning, share a joke from your class joke book.

Art/Writing: Have students design "get well" cards that Ben could send to Alex. Have them decorate the fronts of the cards with pictures of things they think Alex would like. Then have students write messages for Alex on writing paper cut to fit their cards. The messages could be short rhyming couplets, favorite jokes, or simply "get well" messages. Instruct students to glue their messages inside their cards. Display the cards on a bulletin board.

Literature Connection: Share the book *Thinking BIG* by Susan Kuklin (Lothrop, Lee, & Shepard, 1986). It is the true story a girl who is a little person. The book explains how she deals with challenges of independent living. There is also information about accompanying health problems. Have students compare the girl's life with Alex's.

Home Connection

Ask students to look through their games and toys at home to see which ones would be appropriate for children who were in bed recovering from an illness. Write their ideas on chart paper. Then have students draw pictures of their ideas to cut out and decorate the list. Write *Alex's To-Do List* at the top of the paper. Display the list in the classroom.

Activity Sheets

Puzzle Time
Skill Level: Moderate
Have students cut apart puzzle pieces, put them together, and glue them to a backing page.

Puppet Time
Skill Level: Moderate
Have each student draw a puppet character or face on the picture of the paper bag, then write what the puppet might say to Alex.

Comparisons
Skill Level: Difficult
Have students use the correct *-er* form of the word to compare and contrast Alex and Ben.

Name _____

Puzzle Time

One thing Alex could do while getting better is put together a puzzle. Here is a puzzle that Alex might like. Cut out the puzzle pieces. Put them together and glue them to another paper. Color the picture when you are finished.

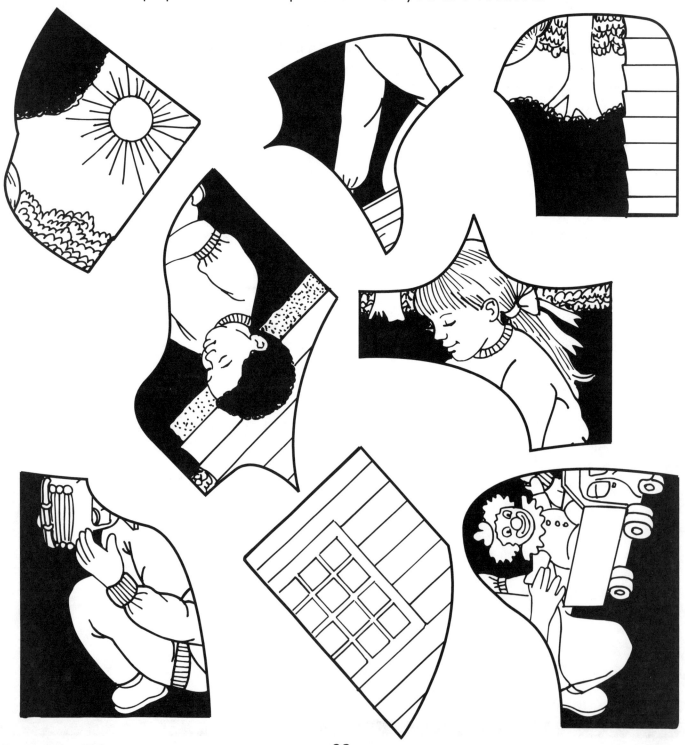

Name _____

Puppet Time

A puppet might cheer up someone who has been sick. Draw a character or face on the paper bag below to make Alex happy.

What is the puppet's name? _____

Write something the puppet might say to Alex.

_____

_____

_____

_____

_____

         Reproducible

Name _____

Comparisons

Read the first part of each question and fill in the blank with the "er" form of the word in parentheses. Then complete the second part of each sentence.

1. Who was _____? (small)

   _____ was _____.
   (Alex or Ben)   (small)

2. Who was _____? (old)

   _____ was _____.
   (Alex or Ben)   (old)

3. Who ran _____? (fast)

   _____ was _____.
   (Alex or Ben)   (fast)

4. Who was _____? (big)

   _____ was _____.
   (Alex or Ben)   (big)

5. Who was _____? (funny)

   _____ was _____.
   (Alex or Ben)   (funny)

Ruby Mae Has Something to Say

by David Small
Publisher: Crown Publishing, 1992
Type: Fiction

Book Summary

Ruby Mae Foote is a small-town politician who overcomes a serious speech disorder by wearing a Bobatron, special headgear invented by her nephew. When the Bobatron is lost before an important speech, Ruby Mae realizes that self-confidence and clear communication skills are far more important than looking good.

Vocabulary

apparatus	decipher	incomprehensible	satellites
apparent	disaster	insulted	talons
colander	emerged	invention	translator
convulsed	flashbulbs	podium	utensils
daunted	humanity	residents	universal

Vocabulary Activity

Print the vocabulary words on chart paper and review them with the class. Then prepare an activity sheet on which you first separate the vocabulary words into syllables, then mix up the syllables for students to decipher. For example:

man-hu-ty-i = _____ (humanity)

You might prompt students by underlining the first syllable.

Discussion Questions

Discuss these questions *before* you read the book with students:

- How would you describe self-confidence?

- How important do you think self-confidence is to success?

- How do you feel when you speak in front of a group? Are you nervous? Are you relaxed?

Discuss these questions *while* you read the book with students:

- Did the Bobatron really make Ruby Mae's speech better? How does the Bobatron work?

- Do you think Ruby Mae could have given her speech if the audience had not started laughing?

Discuss these questions *after* you read the book with students:

- How does Billy Bob help his aunt? What do you think he will be when he grows up? Would you want a friend like Billy Bob?

- What should you do when listening to someone with a speech disorder?

- Which do you think is more important—looking good or speaking plainly? Why do you think that?

Extension Activities

Research/Map Skills: Have students do research about the United Nations. Ask them to find out what it is, where it is located, and in what ways it works for world peace. Students can check a current *World Almanac* to find out which countries are members. Have students select a United Nations country and locate it on a world map.

Class Visitor/Letter Writing: Invite a speech therapist to your class. Have the class read the story about Ruby Mae to the speech therapist. Then let children ask the speech therapist questions. Ask the speech therapist to discuss speech disorders and the ways students can help affected peers. Afterward, have students write a thank-you note to the speech therapist.

Self-esteem: Point out to students that Ruby Mae felt better about her speech because of Billy Bob's contraption. The Bobatron didn't do anything to help Ruby Mae physically, but it boosted her confidence and made her feel better. Brainstorm with students about what boosts their self-confidence. Ask students to complete this sentence starter: "I feel confident when . . ."

Critical Thinking: Discuss with students what it would be like for them to have good ideas that they were unable to express clearly. What are some ways they could get help with this problem?

Home Connection

Ask students to prepare short speeches about world peace. They can practice delivering their speeches at home in front of a mirror and in front of their families. Encourage them to work with their families to design big hats they can wear. If possible, set up a video camera to record students' speeches. Students can view the videotape to watch their speeches.

Activity Sheets

Your Invention
Skill Level: Moderate
Have students draw pictures of original inventions. Students then describe what their inventions do and how they work.

Character Words
Skill Level: Difficult
Have students write character words that describe both Ruby Mae and Billy Bob.

Name _____

Your Invention

Billy Bob made a **Bob**atron.

You can make a _____ atron!
　　　　　　　　　(your name)

Draw your invention
on the easel.

What will your invention do? How does it work? Write about it below.

_____

_____

_____

_____

_____

Reproducible　　　　　　　　　**104**

Name _____

Character Words

What words describe Ruby Mae? Draw a picture of her, then write describing words next to her picture.

What words describe Billy Bob? Draw a picture of him, then write describing words next to his picture.

Manual Alphabet

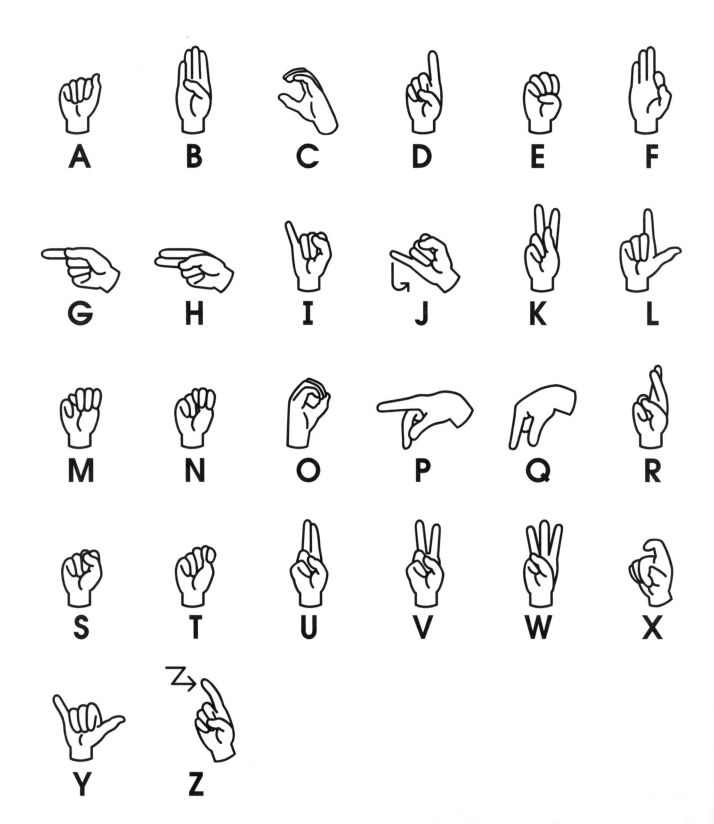

Braille Alphabet

a   b   c   d   e   f   g

h   i   j   k   l   m   n

o   p   q   r   s   t   u

v   w   x   y   z

    Reproducible

Resources

AIDS Action Council
1875 Connecticut Ave. N.W., Suite 700
Washington, DC 20009

American Foundation for the Blind
11 Penn Plaza, Suite 300
New York, NY 10001

American Speech-Language-Hearing Association
10801 Rockville Pike
Rockville, MD 20852

Association for Children with Down Syndrome, Inc.
2616 Martin Avenue
Bellmore, NY 11710

Autism Society of America
7910 Woodmount Avenue, Suite 300
Bethesda, MD 00814-3015

Canine Companions for Independence
P.O. Box 446
Santa Rosa, CA 95402-0446
800-572-BARK

Children and Adults with Attention
    Deficit Disorder
8181 Professional Place, Suite 201
Landover, MD 20785
800-233-4050

Guide Dogs for the Blind, Inc.
P.O. Box 151200
San Rafael, CA 94915-1200
800-295-4050

HELPING HANDS
1505 Commonwealth Ave.
Boston, MA 02135
617-787-4419

National Association for the Deaf
814 Thayer Avenue
Silver Spring, MD 20910-4500

National Attention Deficit
    Disorder Association
P.O. Box 972
Mentor, OH 44061

National Down Syndrome Society
666 Broadway
New York, NY 10012
212-460-9330

Orton Dyslexia Society—Indiana Branch
489-B Gradle Avenue
Carmel, IN 46032

Bibliography

Alex, the Kid with AIDS by Linda Walvoord Girard (Whitman, 1991).

Be Good to Eddie Lee by Virginia Fleming (Philomel, 1993).

Dear Dr. Bell . . . Your Friend, Helen Keller by Judith St. George (Turtleback, 1993).

Different, Not Dumb by Margo Marek (Watts, 1985).

Finger Spelling Fun by David A. Adler (Watts, 1980).

Friends in the Park by Rochelle Bunnett (Checkerboard Press, 1992).

The Handmade Alphabet by Laura Rankin (Dial, 1991).

Helen Keller by Lois Markham (Watts, 1993).

I Have a Sister—My Sister Is Deaf by Jeanne Whitehouse Peterson (HarperCollins, 1977).

I'm Deaf, and It's Okay by Lorraine Aseltine (Whitman, 1987).

Introducing Beethoven by Roland Vernon (Silver Burdett, 1995).

Living with Deafness by Barbara Taylor (Watts, 1989).

Living with Learning Disabilities by David E. Hall (Lerner, 1996).

Loop the Loop by Barbara Dugan (Greenwillow Books, 1992).

Mental and Emotional Disabilities by Jean Dick (Crestwood, 1988).

Michael by Tony Bradman (Macmillan, 1990).

Mom's Best Friend by Sally Hobart Alexander (Macmillan, 1992).

My Great Grandpa by Martin Waddell (Putnam, 1990).

Princess Pooh by Kathleen M. Muldoon (Concept Books, 1989).

Reach for the Moon by Samantha Abeel (Pfeifer-Hamilton, 1994).

Red Ribbon by Sarah Weeks (HarperCollins, 1993).

The Science of Music by Melvin Berger (Thomas Crowell Junior Books, 1989).

Sesame Street Sign Language by Sesame Street Staff (Random House, 1980).

Seven Blind Mice by Ed Young (Philomel, 1992).

Short Stature from Folklore to Fact by Elaine Landau (Watts, 1997).

Thinking BIG by Susan Kuklin (Lothrop, Lee, & Shepard, 1986).

Thumbs Up, Rico! by Maria Testa (Concept Books, 1994).

What Is the Sign for Friend? by Judith E. Greenberg (Watts, 1985).

Where's Chimpy? by Berniece Rabe (Whitman, 1991).

With the Wind by Liz Damrell (Watts, 1991).

Picture Books for an Inclusive Classroom Book Information

Alex Is My Friend by Marisabina Russo (Greenwillow Books, 1992).

Arnie and the New Kid by Nancy Carlson (Puffin, 1992).

The Balancing Girl by Berniece Rabe (Dutton, 1981).

Beethoven Lives Upstairs by Barbara Nichol (Orchard Books, 1994).

A Guide Dog Puppy Grows Up by Caroline Arnold (Harcourt, Brace, Jovanovich, 1991).

Harry and Willy and Carrothead by Judith Caseley (Greenwillow Books, 1991).

Helping Hands by Suzanne Haldane (Dutton Children's Books, 1991).

Imagine Me on a Sit-Ski! by George Moran (Albert Whitman & Company, 1994).

Knots on a Counting Rope by Bill Martin, Jr. and John Archambault (Henry Holt and Company, 1997).

Mom Can't See Me by Sally Hobart Alexander (Macmillan, 1990).

My Buddy by Audrey Osofsky (Henry Holt and Company, 1992).

Our Brother Has Down's Syndrome by Shelley Cairo (Firefly Books, 1985).

Our Teacher's in a Wheelchair by Mary Ellen Powers (Albert Whitman & Company, 1986).

A Picture Book of Helen Keller by David A. Adler (Holiday House, 1991).

Ruby Mae Has Something to Say by David Small (Crown Publishing, 1992).

Russell Is Extra Special: A Book About Autism for Children by Charles A. Amenta III, M.D. (Magination Press, 1992).

Silent Lotus by Jeanne M. Lee (Farrar, Straus, Giroux, 1991).

Summer Tunes: A Martha's Vineyard Vacation by Patricia McMahon (Boyds Mills Press, 1996).

What Do You Mean I Have a Learning Disability? by Kathleen M. Dwyer (Walker and Company, 1991).

What Do You Mean I Have Attention Deficit Disorder? by Kathleen M. Dwyer (Walker and Company, 1996).

Additional Books